Malcolm Shuttleworth
Perfektes Englisch

Malcolm Shuttleworth

Perfektes Englisch

How to improve your English
in 100 easy steps

Anaconda

Special thanks

to Sharon Grimbley,
John White and
Sandrine Leroyer

for proofreading, tips and advice.

Die Deutsche Nationalbibliothek verzeichnet diese Publikation
in der Deutschen Nationalbibliografie; detaillierte bibliografische Daten
sind im Internet unter http://dnb.d-nb.de abrufbar.

Umschlagmotive: iStockphoto.com / © feedough (Hund). –
iStockphoto.com / © visual7 (Flagge)
Umschlaggestaltung: Druckfrei. Dagmar Herrmann, Köln
Satz und Layout: Andreas Paqué, www.paque.de
Printed in Czech Republic 2013
ISBN 978-3-7306-0009-2
www.anacondaverlag.de
info@anacondaverlag.de

Inhalt

Vorwort

How to improve your English in 100 easy steps ist das Ergebnis von zehn Jahren Englischunterricht in deutschen Klassenzimmern. Wenn ich jedes Mal dafür einen Cent bekommen hätte, wenn statt des Verbs „do“ „make“ oder statt „watch“ „look“ benutzt wurde, wäre ich schon längst Millionär. Es gibt unzählige typische Fehler, die deutsche Muttersprachler machen, wenn sie Englisch sprechen. Manche kommen so häufig vor, dass sie schon regelrecht zum Repertoire eines Fremdsprachenschülers gehören.

Ziel dieses Buches ist es, diese Fehler auszumerzen. Es ist ein 100 Lektionen umfassender Leitfaden, mit dem man schrittweise an die vielen Fallen herangeführt wird, in die man beim Englischsprechen gerne tappt: das Benutzen falscher Verben oder Präpositionen, die falsche Anwendung von Ausdrücken oder direktes – und damit meist falsches – Wort-für-Wort-Übersetzen. Hier nur einige Beispiele: *I have an own car*, *we see us tomorrow*, *I have been to the cinema yesterday*, *I was by my mother-in-law*. Diese Sätze sehen vielleicht gut aus, sind aber leider alle falsch!

Lesen Sie einfach mein Buch und ich bin mir sicher, Sie werden sich wundern, wie viel Sie dabei lernen und wie oft Sie feststellen werden, dass Ihnen so mancher der hier vorgestellten Fehler selbst schon oft unterlaufen ist. Am Ende des Buches finden Sie Übungen, die Ihnen dabei helfen sollen, das Gelernte anzuwenden, um so in Zukunft weniger Fehler zu machen.

Ich wünsche Ihnen viel Spaß dabei!
Und vergessen Sie nicht: Do it, don’t make it!

Odenthal im Juni 2013
Malcolm Shuttleworth

Watch out for the grey speech bubbles in this book. They contain typical mistakes.

Corrections are given in the white ones right next to them.

100 tips which will immediately improve your English

1 Don’t make it …

One important thing to remember when speaking English is that nearly every time you say the word **‘make’**, you are ‘making a mistake’! Use **‘do’** instead!

… do it! (1)

‘Make’ is usually used for producing things.

2 Don't look it …

Don't ever use the word **'look'** if something takes a long time, for example a few minutes or hours. Better **'watch'** it!

… watch it!

'Look' is used for things that take a short time, or an instance …

3 Don’t use ‘have’ …

Don’t use **‘have’** with words such as **yesterday**, **last week**, **two years ago** and **last year**.

… use the simple past form of the verb!

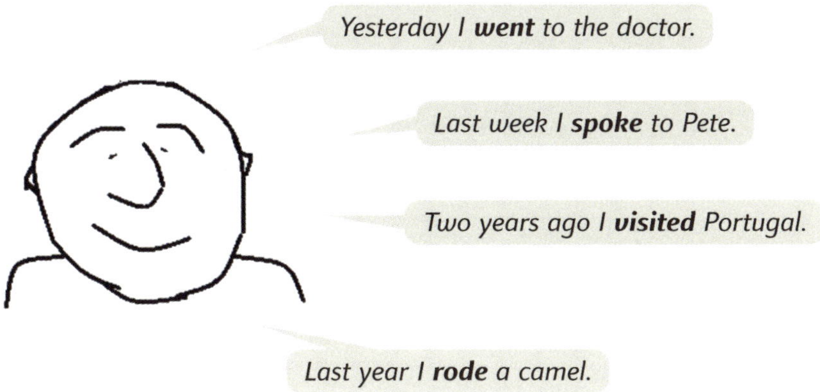

Use **‘have’** only without a fixed time in the past (to say **what** you have done, **not when**!).

4 Don't use 'by' …

Don't use **'by'** if you are talking about **someone you have visited** or if you have been to someone's house. Use **'at'** and **an apostrophe** for the **place**.

… use 'at' and an apostrophe.

*I was at the **doctor's**.*

*I was at my **mother's** house.*

*My wife is staying at her **sister's**.*

*I went round to my **brother's** place.*

Use **'with'** if you are talking about **the person** (not the place).

*I was **with** the doctor.*

*I'm staying **with** my mother.*

*I went on holiday **with** my hairdresser.*

*He's **with** his brother.*

5 Use 'many' if you can count something.

Things that are easy to count are always **countable** and need **'many'**.

Use **'much'** for things you cannot count, or things that are all different shapes and sizes and therefore **difficult to count**.

6 Don't Germanise it! (1)

Try to avoid speaking **Germisch** or **Denglisch**!

7 Don't give uncountable things an article or an '-s'.

Many nouns are **uncountable** (advice, news). They cannot be changed and do not need **an article (a/an)** or an **'-s'**.

Don't add **'s'** to words that are already in the **plural form**.

8 Don't use the wrong vocabulary. (1)

9 Don't mix your countries with your languages! (1)

*When I'm in **Italy** I eat pizza, pasta and olives. I love **Italian** food!*

*In **Spain** it has to be paella. The **Spanish** really know how to cook.*

*Have you seen the breakfast in **England**? Sausage, bacon, eggs, beans, fried bread and mint sauce! **English** breakfast? No, thank you!*

*In **France** they eat frogs' legs and snails! Those **French** will eat anything!*

10 Don't mix adjectives and adverbs.

Remember to use an **adjective** to describe a **noun** and an **adverb** to describe a **verb**.

*A Jack in the box is **funny**.*

*It springs out of the box very **quickly**.*

*Rex is a **good** dog.*

*But he barks **loudly**.*

*Steve is a **nice** boy.*

*He rides his bike **slowly**.*

*Mrs Stick is using a **big** umbrella.*

*Because it is raining **heavily**.*

11 Don’t confuse spelling with pronunciation.

Many words are **hard to pronounce** because they sound nothing like how they are written. Make sure you get their spelling and pronunciation right.

1 Lies „pöhrtschiss“.
2 Lies „pöhrpöss“.

12 Don't forget to get your words in the right order. (1)

There are a couple of words that often appear together in common expressions (black and white). Make sure you put them in the **right order**.

13 Don't mix your nouns and verbs. (1)

*Are you **selling** more?*

*Yes, **sales** have increased!*

*Is that **true**?*

*Yes, I'm **telling the truth**!*

*What about **expansion**?*

*We're **expanding** all the time!*

*If you are unhappy with the deal, we are willing to **negotiate**!*

*No, no! That's ok! There is no need for **negotiation**!*

*What about **manufacturing**?*

*We can **manufacture** more, if you wish?*

*We need more **information** about the South American connection …*

*I will **inform** you about that as soon as I can.*

*What about the new **'product'**?*

***Production** starts next week.*

*Good, Don Cannelloni does not like any **disappointment**!*

*I will do my utmost not to **disappoint** him!*

14 Get your prepositions right!

Are you interested on politics?

Certainly not! I'm interested **in** politics.

I saw you on the party, didn't I?

No you did not! You saw me **at** the party!

Are you good in speaking foreign languages?

No! But I'm good **at** English.

With what age did you get married?

I got married **at** the age of 29.

Did you do the decorating by your own?

No. I did it **on** my own!

Do you get to work by feet?

No. **On** foot actually!

Are you busy at work on the moment?

Well, I'm busy **at** the moment.

15 Don't say too much!

It's 10 o'clock p.m.

You mean **10 p.m.**

We are going on holiday the week after next week.

Really? We are going on holiday **the week after next**.

My husband was given a five-years contract!

They only gave me a **five-year** contract.

You live in the near of Hamburg, don't you?

No, I live **near** Hamburg!

I've had enough, I'm going to home!

I'm just **going home**!

16 Get your expressions right. (1)

17 Say 'bye-bye' to 'by'!

Sometimes when you use **'by'** it might be wrong, especially when you're talking about places.

Do you work by the post office?

*No! I work **at** the post office.*

Were you by your brother?

*No! I was **at** my brother's!*

Were you by the army?

*No! I was **in** the army.*

Do you go to work by feet?

*No! I go **on** foot!*

Were you by the hairdresser?

*No! But I've been **to** the hairdresser's.*

Did you do the work in your flat by your own?

*No! I did it **on** my own.*

Do you have to be at work by seven o'clock?

Yes, that's right!

18 To be or not to be?

Sometimes you need **'to'**, sometimes you don't …

I'm going to home early today.

*Just **go home** early.*

I'm going to holiday in June.

*I'm going **on holiday** in June.*

Shall we go in a pub tonight?

*Yes, but first we have to **go to** the pub!*

What about Bill?
Have you talked at him?

*I've **talked to** him. He's not coming.*

Is he going to jogging again?

*No, he's just **going** jogging!*

19 Don't translate word for word. (1)

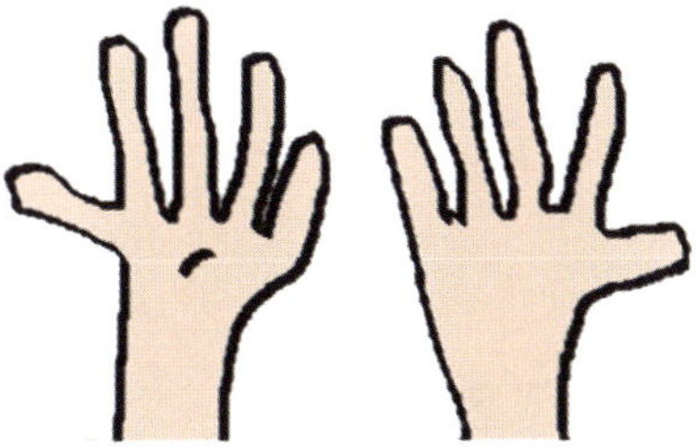

*On the **one hand** it's great, on the **other hand** it's not. (The hands are **side by side**.)*

'On the one side, on the other side' is typical Germisch – don't use it!

*I'm so **happy** and **lucky** to have you!*

Use 'happy' to describe how you feel.
Use 'lucky' if you've had good fortune.

*We made **a big profit** last year because we play to **win.***

Use 'profits' to talk about business and finance. Use 'wins' for sporting achievements. ('We've played five games and had four wins'.)

*I like to **spend money on** my children.*

*It's **for me**!*

Don't mix spend and donate:
Spend money on your children,
donate money to charity.

20 Don’t mix up ‘during’ and ‘while’.

Use **‘while’** with a **verb** and **‘during’** with a **noun**.

21 Look out for 'look after' and 'look for'.

'Look after' and **'look for'** mean different things. So make sure you always use the right one.

22 Watch your prefixes! (1)

Some **prefixes** turn the meaning of a word into its opposite (possible – impossible). Make sure to use the right ones.

23 Use 'there is'/'there was' or 'there are'/'there were' for numbers.

Don't use 'we are' or 'we were' when speaking of **numbers**.
Use **'there is/was'** or **'there are/were'** instead.

24 Don't mix your countries with your languages! (2)

25 Don't mix up your time prepositions.

26 Don't mix 'who' and 'which'!

Use **'who'** for people, **'which'** for things.

A hammer is **something which** you use to hammer in nails.

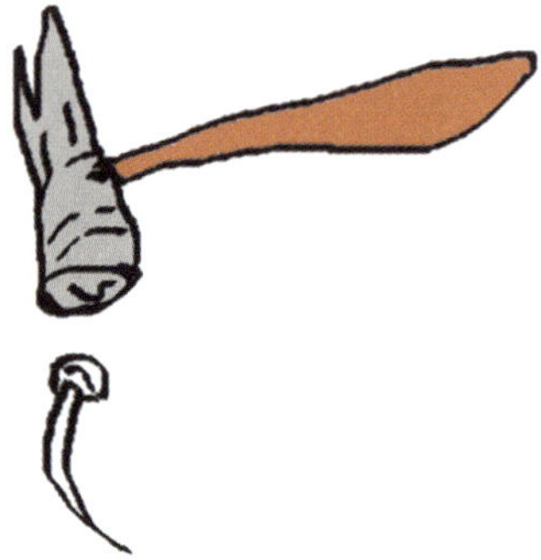

A doctor is **someone who** has to work long hours.

A radio is **something which** has been around for a long time.

A couch potato is **someone who** lazes around all day.

27 Adjective or adverb?

Don't forget to put the **'-ly'** at the end of the **adjective** if you are using it with a **verb**.

28 Use an adverb to describe an adjective.

Add **'-ly'** at the end of the **adjective** and you have the **adverb**.

29 Don't use verbs that don't exist!

Be careful with **irregular verbs**.

30 Don't translate word for word. (2)

She is reading **the menu**,
not the card or the menu card!

He's delivering birthday **cards**. And inside one of them is a **ticket** to the theatre! So leave the cards at home when you go to the theatre, but don't forget your ticket!

When it rains he has to use an umbrella, because it's raining!

If it snows, he'll stay at home. But it might not snow!

31 Use your adjectives correctly.

If you want to describe **something**, use **'-ing'** at the end.

If you want to describe **how someone feels**, use **'-ed'**.

It was a really **relaxing** day …

And the game was **exciting** …

The food was **disgusting** …

32 Use the -ing form for fixed future plans.

Use the **-ing form** of the verb (with a future time) for **fixed future plans**.

33 Don't say 'don't' …

Don't say **'don't'** with **he**, **she** and **it**.
For the **third person singular** use **'doesn't'** instead.

… for the third person singular (another person or thing).

34 Don’t Germanise it! (2)

Love is **all** … … but money isn’t **everything**.

He loves **to travel**.

Remember: travel is what it’s all about, but you go on individual journeys or trips.

35 Don't use the wrong verbs. (1)

Some nouns only go together with certain verbs. For example, there are things you can only ride and others that you can drive.

Ride what you can sit on …

Ride a horse.

Ride a donkey.

Ride a bike.

Drive what you get into …

Drive a car.

Drive a bus
(if you're the bus driver.)

Take public transport.

Take the bus or the train or a taxi (let the taxi driver drive the taxi!)

36 Don't Germanise it! (3)

You can **cook meat** … but remember to **boil water** to **make coffee**.

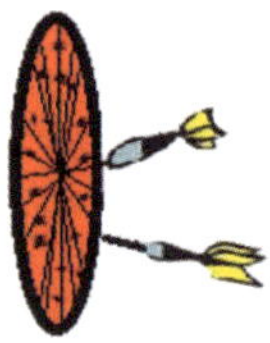

Use **a dart** to play **darts**.

Enjoy **life** … but watch **live** music.

37 Don't use the wrong verbs. (2)

Make a cup of tea …

… but **take** a photograph.

Make a cake …

… but **go on** holiday.

Spend money on new clothes …

… but **donate** to charity.

38 Don't confuse your words.

Some words are easy to confuse because they sound almost the same or are spelled very similar.
But that doesn't mean that they have the same meaning.

39 Get your prepositions right at home.

Where did you see him first?

***On** TV.*

Where did you hear his new song?

***On** the radio.*

Where's that pop magazine?

***On** the shelf.*

Where are the pictures of your ex-boyfriend?

***In** the bin.*

Where will you hang your new heartthrob's picture?

***On** my bedroom wall.*

40 Don't mix 'do you' and 'would you'.

Use **'do you'** to ask about people's preferences,
use **'would you'** to ask if someone wants something.

41 Use '-ing' with preference verbs.

Combine **preference verbs** with the **-ing form** (I **like**, **love**, **hate doing** something).

42 Prove, proof or check?

Prove that something is correct.
Provide **proof** or **evidence** to catch a criminal.
Check that something is in working order.

Always **check your tyres** before a long car journey …

43 Use simple present or present perfect correctly.

Use the **simple present** for normal, fixed things.

Use the **present perfect** for time periods until now.

44 Don't use 'with' for ages, use 'at' instead (at the age of).

I said my first word **at the age of 0**.

I fell in love
at the age of six.

I got married **at 26**.

I became a granddad **at 52**.

45 Don't say 'hear' or 'listen', say 'listen to'.

You **'hear'** something for a little while.
('Can you hear the wind blowing?')
But you **'listen to'** something for a longer time.
'Listen' is a command - 'listen to me!'

You can **listen to** the radio.

You can **listen to** your neighbours.

You should **listen to** your mother.

You can **listen to** the football results.

46 Be sure when to use 'say' and 'tell'?

Remember the golden rule, you **say something** but you **tell someone** something.

47 Don't use the wrong words.

Food is prepared in the kitchen, the **kitchen** must be clean.

You **borrow** money from a bank, the bank **lends** it to you.

48 We just don't say that! (1)

49 Don't confuse your words. (1)

*I am trying **quite** hard to be **quiet**.*

*Well, that's **hardly** very **hard**!*

*Help! I've got 10 **diners** coming for **dinner** in 10 minutes!*

*If I didn't **spend** so much money on myself, I'd **donate** some to charity.*

50 Don't forget to get your words in the right order. (2)

51 Get your prepositions right in the office.

*Mr Alfter is **on the phone** at the moment.*

*Mr Podien will be available shortly. I think he's just about to **hang up**!*

*Mr Owen and Mr Collins are **in** an important meeting.*

The bad news is that's just my bank balance!

52 Don't use the -ing form to talk about regular, fixed things in your life!

53 Don't confuse your words. (2)

Remember, it is not always **safe** to **save** your money in a **safe**!

After a **week** of hiking he felt very **weak**.

An **alcoholic** has a problem with **alcohol**.

54 Have a stab at the past perfect.

To use the **past perfect** you start your sentence talking about the past, then you go **even further into the past**.

The past	Before that
*When I **got home** last night …*	*… someone **had broken** my window.*

*When I **left** the vicarage yesterday …*

*… someone **had stolen** my bicycle!*

*When I **got up** this morning …*

*… the dog **had eaten** my slippers!*

55 Don’t mix ‘by’ and ‘until’.

Use **‘until’** to talk about **how much longer** you have to do something.

Use **‘by’** for **deadlines**.

56 'Of' or 'from'?

'Of' and **'from'** always cause problems. Try to remember these basics.

It's a matter **of** time …

The coach **of** the football team has a problem …

57 Don't forget the '-s'! (1)

This may come as a surprise, but all the following expressions need an **'-s'**!

58 Don't use an 's' when it's not necessary!

Some words **DO NOT** need an **'s'**! So leave them alone.

59 Don’t say ‘an own’.

When you talk about possessions or owners use **a possessive pronoun** (his/her/their/our/my/your).

60 When do I use what? (1)

Part-time or half-time?

*My brother's got a **part-time** job reading the **half-time foot-ball results** on the local radio.*

Fly or flight?

*People who hate **flying** never enjoy the **flight.***

Will we crash? Will we get hijacked? Will we run out of fuel?

Game or play?

*It's only a **game**, but you have to **play** fair.*

*My **boss** is a great **chef**! He **cooks** really well!*

Chef or boss?

61 We just don't say that! (2)

62 Don't use 'a' or 'an'.

Remember many words are **uncountable**, they don't need **'a'** or **'an'**. You can talk about the weather but never about 'a' weather.

Let's talk about **the weather**.

It's either **good weather**.

Or it's **bad weather**.

That's it!

Let's talk about **food**.

Apple**s**, pear**s**, biscuit**s** and orange**s**.

We can count them.

But what are they collectively?

Food.

What have we here?

A loaf and lots of rolls.

All types of **bread**.

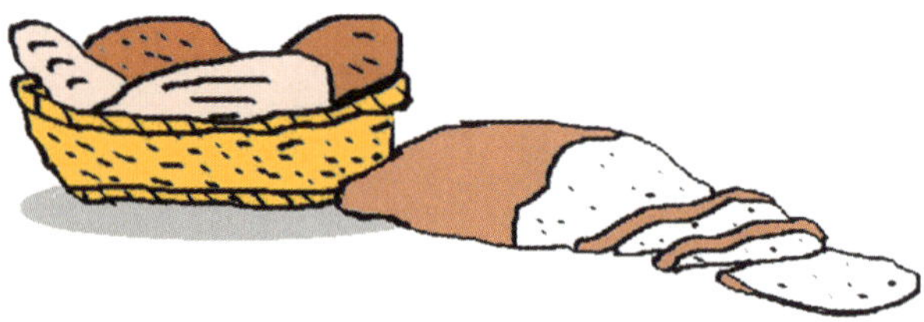

63 Don't confuse your words. (3)

Wake up in the morning,
get up (out of bed),
but **stand up** if you don't
want to **sit down** anymore!

He calls himself **an artist**
and says he lives for **his art**.
But not many people
like **his style**!

64 Don't confuse 'same as' or 'like' or 'than'?

Many people mix these expressions up. Remember:

If two things are the **same**, you can say
'it's **the same as** …' or 'it's **like** …' (It's **the same as** yesterday).

If two things are **different**, use '**than**' (I'm bigger **than** you!).

65 Don't mix your nouns and verbs. (2)

*The boss said they are worried about **production**.*

*Why don't they **produce** more then?*

*Well, it's a **combination** of two things.*

*Laziness **combined** with greed?*

*No. The machines are hard to **maintain** and the **products** are hard to handle.*

*They should outsource **maintenance**, it's cheaper. Have they **decided** what to do?*

*No, but I think they will reach a **decision** soon.*

*I blame the **management**. They don't know how to **manage**!*

66 Don't Germanise it! (4)

67 Get your seasons and holidays right!

Every June he **goes on holiday**.

She gets lots of eggs **at Easter**.

It always snows **in winter**.

He has a lot to do **at Christmas**.

68 Get your expressions right! (2)

That was a great documentation.

It was ***a documentary****, dear!*

Why do you always have to mention my failures?

I only correct your ***mistakes****, my dear!*

I'm speaking more English in my actual job.

You mean your ***current*** *job!*

Would you like to go and sleep in the floor?

No! I'm not going to sleep ***in the corridor*** *either!*

Only joking! Can you bring me to the airport tomorrow?

No. But I can ***take you*** *to the airport!*

69 Have a stab at the past progressive.

The **-ing form** of the verb is used for temporary situations, what you are doing now (I am working), what is happening in your life at the moment (I'm reading a good book at the moment), and what you were doing in the past **at a particular time, for a short period of time** (past progressive: Yesterday at this time **I was watching** the game).

At the moment Sally is working, but she's not happy.

Things are not going well for Steve's team this season …

… **this time last year** they were lifting the cup.

John is depressed …

70 ‘Don’t’, ‘doesn’t’, ‘didn’t’ or ‘not’? Always use the right form.

‘Don’t’ is used with I/you/we/they in the **simple present**.

‘Doesn’t’ is used for the **third person singular** (he, she, it).

‘Didn’t’ is used for the **past negative** (for everyone).

‘Not’ is used with **the present progressive** and with **adjectives**.

71 Get your tenses right.

Try to remember **the absolute basics**:
How to form the different **tenses** and when to use which.

You need **is/am/are** and the **-ing form** of the verb to describe what's happening **now**.

*Little Joey **is riding** a bike.*

*Old Ned **is singing**.*

*Stevie **is running**.*

You need the **infinitive** for things that happen **all the time** and **the s form** of the verb for the **third person singular**. You need **doesn't** for the third person negative.

*Little Joey **rides** every day.*

*Old Ned **sings** in a club every Saturday night.*

*Stevie **runs** everywhere!*

*Little Joey **doesn't ride** to school, he takes the bus.*

*Old Ned **doesn't sing** modern songs, he prefers oldies.*

*Stevie **doesn't run** in the rain.*

You need the **present perfect progressive** (have/has + been + the -ing form of the verb) to talk about **how long** someone **has been doing** something.

*Little Joey **has been riding a bike** since he was three.*

*Old Ned **has been singing** since he was a child.*

*Stevie **has been running** since he could walk!*

72 Watch your plurals!

In most cases you can create the plural form simply by adding an **s** at the end of the singular form (cat – cat**s**). But watch out for the irregular plural forms!

Ok, Mr Westermann, you have 30 seconds on your chosen specialist subject ***'plurals'*** *starting … now. The plural form of* ***child*** *is …*

Errr, ***children****!*

Correct! One mouse. Two …

Mouses?

Wrong, two ***mice****. The plural form of woman is …*

Women*!*

Correct! One sheep, two …

Sheeps?

No. Two ***sheep****! One person, many …*

Hmmm, ***people****!*

Correct! One goose, several …

Gooses?

No, ***geese****! The plural form of furniture is …*

There isn't one – ***furniture****!*

Correct! One man, two …

Men*!*

Correct! And you've run out of time, but you've scored five ***points****!*

73 'Too many' or 'too much'?

It's those horrible countables and uncountables again! Remember, if it's hard to count, if you can't see it or if it's all different shapes and sizes, it's uncountable – then you have to use **'much'**, not **'many'**!

It's all **too much** …

money

traffic

knowledge

How **many**?

Too many cooks …

74 Get your spelling right! (1)

Many singular nouns have **f** at the end or near the end of the word, these words are usually spelt with **v** in the **plural form**.

75 'A' or 'an' – remember the exceptions to the rules!

The rules for using **'a'** or **'an'** are mostly straightforward. Generally you use **'an'** before a word beginning with **a vowel** (a, e, i, o, u) and **'a'** before a word beginning with a consonant (b, c, d, f, etc.). But there are exceptions. Take a look:

76 Don't make it!

'Make' is the most misused verb. Don't **make** any of these things!

Do advertising

Do market research

Go on holiday

Do housework

Do your job

77 What can I make?

Make is mostly used for producing things. You can **make** the following:

You can **make a mistake**

2 + 5 = 8 ✗

You can **make a shopping list**

milk
cheese
tomatoes
apples
chicken
flour
potatoes
sage
lettuce
jam
cream

You can **make an appointment**

1	2	3	4	5
6	7	8	9	10
11	12	13	14	15
16	17	18	19	20
21	22	23	24	25
26	27	28	29	30

You can **make a sandwich**

You can **make a cup of coffee**

But remember:

You don't make a party – you **have a party**.
You don't make your work – you **do your work**.

78 Get your tags right!

Tag questions serve to confirm a statement and usually follow the assumption expressed. They are mainly straightforward, but sometimes tricky. Mostly if the question is positive, the tag is negative and vice versa – hence 'You like Tom, **don't you**?' or 'You don't like Tom, **do you**?'

He wouldn't, **would he?**

Little Barbara is beautiful, **isn't she?**

79 Don't forget the '-s'! (2)

The biggest mistake is definitely forgetting the **'-s'** when using the **third person singular**, but don't forget to add **'-s'** when using **plurals** (one of my teacher**s** – plays dart**s** – a friend of our**s** …).

80 When do I use what? (2)

81 Use reflexive pronouns correctly.

~~I remember me … we see us … she loves her …~~

Take all these useless phrases and throw them in the bin!!! 'I remember' and 'see you' don't need reflexive pronouns. 'She loves herself' does. Here are some more examples to remember …

She loves **herself**.

He has hurt **himself**.

They are gossiping amongst **themselves**.

He's talking to **himself**.

82 Use 'by' in the correct way.

You can use **'by'** for measurements, deadlines, songs and books and much more …

A home **by** the sea

83 What do my biggest mistakes look like?

These pictures show you what your mistakes would look like if taken literally. Try to work out which **'false friends'** are represented here. Answers below.

1.

2.

3.

4.

5.

1. What is he doing **on** TV again?
(Was macht der schon wieder im Fernsehen?)
2. I **got** a steak. (Ich habe ein Steak bekommen.)
3. Oh no! They've put the label on **the back!**
(O nein! Das Etikett ist auf der Rückseite.)
4. I prefer sitting in the **shade**. (Ich sitze lieber im Schatten.)
5. What's wrong with my **watch**? (Was ist bloß mit meiner Uhr los?)

84 'Lay', 'lie' or 'lie'?

85 Use an adjective to describe verbs that deal with senses.

Normally **adverbs** are used to describe verbs – I drive carefully, for example.

But this is not the case with verbs that deal with **senses**, therefore something **smells nice**, **feels good**, **looks wonderful,** etc.

86 Use the will future correctly.

Don't use **will future** for **future fixed plans**, use the -ing form of the verb in these cases instead (**I am going** to Spain next Friday).

Use **will future** at the moment you make a decision (Ok, I **will** come with you!), when you are unsure about something (**Maybe** I **will** come with you), or for making predictions (I think it **will** rain!).

87 Place your frequency adverbs right!

Frequency adverbs (sometimes, never, always, seldom, usually, rarely, often, etc.) are best placed **before the verb**.

'Sometimes' is **the only one** of these words that can be placed **at the beginning or end** of the sentences (**sometimes** I play football, I **sometimes** play football, I play football **sometimes**). You cannot do this with the others. So the best place to put the frequency adverbs is **before** the verb.

If you use an auxiliary verb (do, have, can, would, etc.), the adverb should go between the two verbs (I **don't** always **eat** meat).

88 Get your adjectives in the right order.

If you use more than one adjective when describing a noun use the following sequence: **your opinion** followed by **fact**, for example: an **old** lady, a **nice**, **old** lady, a **lazy** man, a **fat**, **lazy** man.

89 Dispense with 'the' when it's not needed.

Words that **do not** generally need **'the'**:
children, music, business, names of most roads, parks, universities, airports and shops and banks named after the people who started them (Lloyds Bank, Macy's, Harrods, etc.).

Words that **do** generally need **'the'**:
hotels, restaurants, theatres, cinemas and museums.

90 Watch your prefixes! (2)

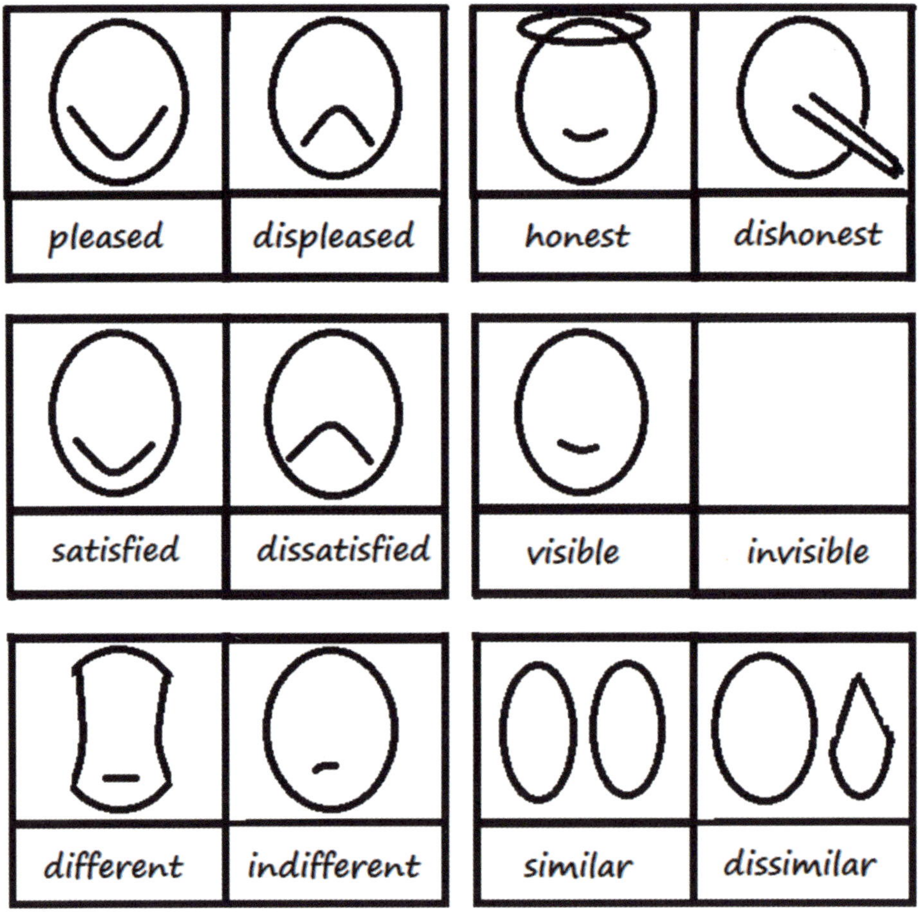

91 Get your apostrophes right.

The use of the apostrophe is very important in the English language. We use an apostrophe to indicate that something or someone **belongs to** or **is connected to someone/something**.

Use **'s** after single nouns (**boy's**) and plural nouns (**men's**) and **s'** after plural nouns ending in **'-s'** (**parents'**).

92 Get your spelling right. (2)

Verbs and nouns that end with the letter **y** sometimes have **different endings** when you use the third person singular (he/she/it) or when you use the plural.

Spelling rule: If the **y** is preceded by a vowel (a, e, i, o, u) add **s** to the words (examples: pl**ay** – pl**ays**, b**oy** – b**oys**). But if the **y** is preceded by a consonant (b, c, d, f, etc.) you have to replace the **y** with the **-ies ending** (examples: t**ry** – t**ries**, count**ry** – count**ries**.).

93 Use the right comparative forms.

We use **'-er'** for short words with one syllable (strong – strong**er**). For longer words with two syllables or more we use **'more'** (terrible – **more** terrible).

big – bigg**er**, small – small**er** …

serious – **more** serious, expensive – **more** expensive …

94 'To', 'too' or 'two' – choose carefully!

Use **to** for movement or travel (he's going **to** bed, she's going **to** Spain).

Use **too** as another form of **also** (I'm going, too.)
and for excess (he's **too** fat!).

Two is used for numbers, figures or amounts
(We made a profit of **twenty-two** percent).

95 Get your travel prepositions right.

Travel **to** a country but when you're there travel **in** or **around** the country.

You can be **in** the airport or **at** the airport but not **on** the airport. (It's illegal!)

You can go **on** foot but **by** bike. You get **on** a bus but **in** a car.

Arrive **at** your destination.

You can be **at** home, but you just go home.

Harry waited for a long time on the airport …

96 Don't forget your past tense.

Remember:

I **have to** (now/in the future)	I **can** (now)	I **must** (now/in the future)
I **had to** (in the past)	I **could** (in the past)	I **had to** (in the past)

97 Have a stab at the present perfect.

The **present perfect** is perhaps the most difficult tense to understand and use, because it can be used in so many different ways. Try to remember:

- You **CANNOT** use the present perfect with time expressions such as yesterday, one year ago or last week, etc.
- You **CAN** use the present perfect with expressions like ever, several times, already, just, for and since.

General grammar rules:

		have/has	+	past participle (the third form of the verb)
I/you/we/they	+	**have**	+	**done/played/been, etc.**
he/she/it	+	**has**	+	**done/played/been, etc.**

98 'There' or 'their'? Always use the right word!

Use **'there'** in general and for places.
Only use **'their'** for people's possessions.

There are five hotels in town.

Your coat is over **there**.

It's **their** car.

The family holiday

99 Don't use an article for things that have two parts.

Objects that have **two parts** do not need an article ('a' or 'an'.)
We say **jeans** or **a pair of jeans**. (**Do not** say 'a jeans' or 'a shorts'.)

Examples include:

trousers/jeans *shorts* *pyjamas* *glasses* *scissors*

100 Avoid making the biggest mistakes!

And now … **the final word** from the Bard of Germisch …

Don't say make, say ***do***
For the things at work, to name not few
Don't say look, say ***watch***
For things like sport which are top-notch
Don't Germanise *your speech*
Practice what you preach
Don't forget ***the '-s'***
For he and she and it, no less

Never use the ***'the'***
For streets and parks, but you can use an ***'a'****!*
Use your ***adverbs*** *well*
To say how things move and go but not smell!
Keep your ***prepositions*** *intact*
Go to or at or from or back

Watch out for those ***countable nouns***
They all need an article of great renown
Now I bid you farewell and my leave I must take
I ask you not to make ***those silly mistakes****!*

Exercises

Remember: The idea of these exercises is not just to fill in verbs, words, etc., but to practise using the words in the correct way. Before you use a verb, think about which form of the verb you need. For example, if the infinitive is 'work', do you need work, worked, works, working, etc.? If you are using a noun, does it need an article? If so, which article (a, an, the, my, etc.)? Is it a plural noun? Does it need s or not?

Have fun! And **think twice** before you write down your answers!

1. 'Do', 'make' or 'have'?

Complete the sentences by using the correct form of 'do', 'make' or 'have'.

1. _____ you like basketball?
2. I think he ______ a good job.
3. I'm getting tired, let's ________ some coffee to wake us up!
4. Are you ________ a party on your birthday?
5. Do you _______ much business with Japan?
6. They are ___________ some work on the street outside.
7. Who is ________ so much noise?
8. I'm hungry, let's _______ something to eat.
9. Tom ______ all the gardening yesterday.
10. Have you ________ your homework?
11. Dad can't come to the phone, he is _______ the housework.
12. I can't believe I ________ so many mistakes in my test!
13. Have you ever _______ a fancy dress party?
14. They are ________ a huge cake for Dad's birthday.
15. I _______ my maths homework yesterday.
16. I always ______ my housework on Friday afternoon.
17. Did you ________ an appointment with the doctor?
18. Have you ever _________ Turkish pizza?
19. Did you ______ a nice holiday?
20. I don't like ___________ nothing, I get bored.

2. 'Look' or 'watch'?

Complete the sentences using the correct form of 'look' or 'watch'.

1. Are you __________ at me?
2. Are you __________ me?
3. Do you ______ a lot of sport on TV?
4. ________ at that man! He's kicking his dog!
5. I __________ the game last night.
6. Bill __________ at the photo for a few seconds.
7. Did you _________ the film last night?
8. I am ___________ for my watch, have you seen it?
9. I sometimes ___________ documentaries on TV.
10. Stop ___________ at your watch all the time!
11. Jack likes ____________ wrestling on TV.
12. The kids are playing hide and seek, they are __________ for each other.
13. ________ at the time! I must be going.
14. Hey, _______ where you are going!
15. Sue ___________ winter sport in the evening.
16. Don't disturb me, I'm __________ my favourite programme.
17. I'm ___________ for a new job.
18. Paul was ___________ for his dog when I saw him last night.
19. I fell asleep while I was __________ the debate.
20. Goodbye, _________ after yourself.

3. When and how to use 'have'

Decide if the following sentences are right or wrong, if you think they are wrong, correct them, as in the examples.

1. I have been to the cinema yesterday.	Wrong! I **went** to the cinema yesterday.
2. I have been to Spain many times.	Right!
3. Paul gone to lunch, he'll be back soon.	______________________________

4. I has made a birthday cake for Helen. ____________________
5. Pete has went to Spain. ____________________
6. I have eaten Sushi many times. ____________________
7. Did you has a good time? ____________________
8. I have watched the game on Sunday. ____________________
9. I eaten my lunch at twelve. ____________________
10. Steve has already did his homework. ____________________
11. I did my housework on Friday. ____________________
12. Are you has a party on Friday? ____________________
13. Did you has a good holiday? ____________________
14. I'm having a break. ____________________
15. She has been to the doctor's. ____________________
16. I went to work on Saturday. ____________________
17. I'm have a day off tomorrow. ____________________
18. Steve had two days off after his crash. ____________________
19. Has you any brothers and sisters? ____________________
20. They has no idea what they are doing! ____________________

4. 'At' or 'with'?

Use 'at' or 'with' to finish these sentences.

1. I was ______ my sister's.
2. He is living ______ Pete until he finds his own place.
3. She was ______ the hairdresser's for hours!
4. He's over forty, but he still lives ______ his parents!
5. I am not sure where he is, I think he's ______ his brother.
6. She's ______ the doctor's.
7. He's gone on holiday ______ his parents.
8. She is living ______ him.
9. I am staying ______ Jill while my flat is being renovated.
10. She's ______ Phil, I think!

5. 'Many' or 'much'?

a. Put the words in the box into two groups, 'how many' or 'how much'.

meat	children	sand	people	hands	feet	progress	men
money	traffic	work	jobs	homework	housework	teeth	roads

how many	how much
______________	______________
______________	______________
______________	______________
______________	______________
______________	______________
______________	______________
______________	______________
______________	______________

b. Complete the sentences using 'many' or 'much'.

1. How __________ progress did you make in the meeting?
2. Does your English teacher give you _______ homework?
3. How ______ housework do you have to do this weekend?
4. Paul put too ________ sand in with the concrete mix.
5. There is always so ______ traffic on the motorways.
6. How ______ children do you have?
7. How ______ jobs does she have?
8. How _____ money will you need to buy the house?
9. How _____ men were needed for the work?
10. How ______ work did you do on the house on Sunday?

6. Don't Germanise it!

Decide if the following sentences are right or wrong, if you think they are wrong, correct them, as in the examples.

1. I need an electriker. Wrong! I need an **electrician**.
2. See you tomorrow! Right!
3. Mum said me I was good. ____________________
4. How was your travel to France? ____________________
5. One of my friend is ill. ____________________
6. Are you good in tennis? ____________________
7. I was on a party last night. ____________________
8. There's Steve!
   He's the husband of my sister. ____________________
9. Let's have a party! ____________________
10. Tom's on a meeting. ____________________

7. Countable or uncountable?

Write down the plural form of the words.

man	____________	woman	____________
child	____________	road	____________
knowledge	____________	information	____________
bread	____________	roll	____________
knife	____________	person	____________
keyboard	____________	advice	____________
homework	____________	news	____________

8. Vocabulary

a. Translate the German words into English.

Spülmaschine	____________	Waschmaschine	____________
sympathisch	____________	Beratung	____________
Aufenthalts-erlaubnis	____________	Mutterschafts-urlaub	____________
Hochzeitstag	____________	Kindergeld	____________
Mehrwertsteuer	____________	Fangfrage	____________

b. Use the English words to complete the sentences. Each word can only be used once.

1. If you need good financial ________, ask Bob.
2. She spends all the ______ ________ on herself!
3. The rate of __________ has gone up again.
4. When is your _________ ___________?
5. Is that a _________ ___________?
6. My __________ ___________ runs out at the end of the year.
7. Is your boss _________?
8. The ________ ________ is broken, I don't have any clean clothes!
9. The ____________ is full.
10. She took 12 months __________ __________ after her son was born.

9. Countries & languages

Write the nationalities next to the countries.

Belgium	____________	Russia	____________
Holland	____________	Canada	____________
Spain	____________	Italy	____________
Iceland	____________	Pakistan	____________
Israel	____________	Kenya	____________

10. Adjectives and adverbs

Use the words in brackets (in the correct form) to complete the sentences, as in the example.

Tom is a really ______ driver, he drives ______. (careful)

Tom is a really careful driver, he drives carefully.

1. I like him, he's __________. (nice)
2. She sings so ____________. (beautiful)
3. The match was so __________. (exciting)

4. Are you __________? (tired)
5. He spoke very __________ to the children. (nice)
6. She shouted __________ at the child. (loud)
7. We completed the deal __________. (successful)
8. He ran home __________. (quick)
9. He stretched __________. (tired)
10. Are you sitting __________? (comfortable)

11. Word order

Take a word from box A and a word from box B to complete the sentences, as in the example.

Box A	
sisters	cats
white	queens
gentlemen	girls
cheese	poor
outs	pots

Box B	
ladies	boys
dogs	**brothers**
ins	pans
black	rich
kings	chalk

1. Do you have any **brothers** and **sisters**?
2. They are so different, they are like ______ and ________!
3. It doesn't matter if you are ________ or ________, just be healthy.
4. ______________ and ____________, welcome to the show!
5. Who is going to clean all the ______ and ________?
6. She is so nosy, she wants to know the ______ and ________ of everything!
7. That film is old, it's in ______ and ________.
8. The ______ and ______ have gone out to play.
9. It's raining ________ and ____________.
10. I like reading novels about ________ and ______ of old England.

12. Nouns and verbs

a. Complete the chart.

Noun	Verb
	(to) protect
mixture	
	(to) correct
	(to) provide
taxation	
imagination	
	(to) prove
composition	
difference	
description	

b. Use some of the words in the chart (in the correct form) to complete the following sentences, as in the example.

If you want to be different, use your **imagination**.

1. The police knew he was guilty, but they couldn't __________ it.
2. 45 % _______ on salaries is too high.
3. Tom got his test back from the teacher and it was full of __________.
4. All our production workers have to wear goggles for __________.
5. Does your company __________ any leisure facilities?
6. John has just __________ a new song.
7. We couldn't agree, so we agreed to __________!
8. _______ the cement in a bucket.
9. The officers have a good __________ of the criminal.
10. She is always __________ my English!

13. General prepositions

Complete the sentences using the correct preposition.

1. I am very good ____ badminton.
2. She got married ____ the age of 25.
3. He's married ____ a model.
4. Let's go to the hotel ____ foot.
5. My kitchen is 8 metres ____ 3 metres.
6. Can you look ____ my dog for a week?
7. I have to finish this job ____ Friday.
8. My hometown is west ____ Manchester.
9. ____ the short-term it's a bad plan.
10. Why not go ____ your own?

14. Don't say too much

Decide if the following sentences are right or wrong, if you think they are wrong, correct them, as in the example.

I live in the near of Hamburg. Wrong! I live **near** Hamburg.

1. He's staying in a five-stars hotel. ________________
2. She has a two-years-old child. ________________
3. It is almost 10 o'clock p.m. ________________
4. He was given a five-year contract. ________________
5. Are you going for a lunch with Jack? ________________
6. Our hotel has five stars. ________________
7. He's coming the month after next. ________________
8. Are you going home? ________________
9. Did you go to the work yesterday? ________________
10. We had a breakfast in bed. ________________

15. Get your expressions right

Answer the following questions using the words in brackets, in the correct form, as in the example.

What do you do when you have any spare money? (spend/clothes)	I **spend it** on clothes.
1. What do you usually do on a Sunday morning? (lie)	______________
2. What do most people do during the week? (up/work)	______________
3. What do you do when you're hungry? (make/eat)	______________
4. How do you keep fit? (sport)	______________
5. What do you do when you are feeling lazy? (nothing)	______________

16. 'At' or 'by'?

Use 'at' or 'by' to complete these sentences.

1. We saw him _____ the cinema.
2. Have you been _____ the hairdresser's?
3. We went _____ taxi.
4. He's _____ his mother's.
5. He's staying _____ a really nice hotel.
6. Do you live ____ the river?
7. He should be here _____ now!
8. _____ the way, you still owe me €50!
9. He did it all _____ himself.
10. _____ the time I get to Phoenix, she'll be sleeping.

17. To be or not to be?

Decide if the following sentences are right. Correct them, if you think they are wrong, as in the example.

I had to go to the doctor yesterday. Right!

1. Did you go to work yesterday? ______________________
2. When are you going to home? ______________________
3. Did you go to holiday last summer? ______________________
4. Shall we go to a nice restaurant tonight? ______________________
5. I'm going to bed. ______________________

18. Don't translate word for word

Complete the sentences by using the correct words.

1. On the one ______, it's a great idea. On the other ______, it's dangerous.
2. The banks make huge __________ at the expense of their customers.
3. I always __________ money to Oxfam at Christmas.
4. Do you __________ a lot of money ________ birthday presents?
5. You found €50? You are so __________.
6. I am __________ with my figure.
7. Did you _______ my message?
8. What has _________ of Tom? I haven't seen him for months!
9. Put the address on the ____________ of the parcel, too!
10. Are you any good _____ chess?

19. 'During' and 'while'

Complete the sentences using 'during' or 'while', as in the example.

I fell asleep **while** watching the film.

1. He learned a lot ________ his time in the army.
2. I like to drink a glass of wine _______ I'm cooking.
3. The telephone rang _______ I was having a shower.
4. When I saw Tom he was waiting for a bus _______ he was reading a book.
5. _______ the conference I did a lot of networking.
6. Will you visit Harry _______ your US trip?
7. Don't talk _______ you're eating.
8. They repair your shoes _______ you wait.

9. I relaxed ________ the weekend.
10. I can't sleep ________ the day.

20. 'Look after' and 'look for'?

Finish the sentences using the correct form of 'look for' or 'look after', as in the example.

Look **after yourself** on your journey.

1. Sue is fed up at work, she is ________________ a new job.
2. He always ____________ the cheapest hotels.
3. He ________________ a new flat last week.
4. I'm ________________ my parents' dog while they are in France.
5. I ____________ the best deals on the internet.
6. He ____________________ his health.
7. I'm ________________ my cat, have you seen it?
8. He ______________ his mother for two years when she was sick.
9. They really ______________ their customers.
10. I've ______________ for my keys everywhere. I can't find them!

21. Prefixes

Turn these words into the negative form by adding the correct prefix, as in the example.

possible	**impossible**	modest	____________
polite	____________	regular	____________
secure	____________	safe	____________
mobile	____________	trustworthy	____________
appear	____________	expected	____________
well	____________	attractive	____________
relevant	____________	able	____________
organised	____________	treated	____________
believable	____________	happy	____________

responsible	___________	mature	___________
sure	___________	reasonable	___________

22. 'There is'/'there are'

Finish the sentences by adding 'there is'/'there are', 'there was'/'there were', as in the examples.

There were 30 people waiting at the check-in.
There are 10 new pupils in my class.

1. _________ no point waiting, he'll be another three hours.
2. I know where _________ more biscuits!
3. She said _________ many problems in her relationship.
4. _________ a lot of dogs in the park.
5. I know _________ something going on!
6. _________ only one till open at the check-out yesterday.
7. _________ a lot of noise coming from Joe's room.
8. _________ thunderstorms last night.
9. _________ not enough hotels in the city.
10. _______________ no infrastructure in our country.

23. Time prepositions

Insert the correct preposition. (Sometimes no preposition is necessary.)

1. Shall we have a party _____ my birthday?
2. We can meet _____ next Tuesday.
3. I saw Bob _____ last week.
4. I play tennis _____ Sunday.
5. I have been working here _____ 10 years.
6. Did you go to church _____ Easter Sunday?
7. Did it snow _____ Christmas?
8. The cat always goes out _____ night.
9. Did you see your mother _____ Christmas Day?
10. The ambulance arrived _____ five minutes.

24. 'Who' and 'which'

Describe the following things using 'who' or 'which', as in the example.

a teacher	a bat	smoking	your best friend	**a nurse**
steak	history	chess	a policeman	a car

1. **A nurse** is someone **who** looks after sick people.
2. ____
3. ____
4. ____
5. ____
6. ____
7. ____
8. ____
9. ____
10. ____

25. Using an adverb to describe an adjective

Use two words from the box, in the correct form, to describe the things below, as in the example. (More than one variation is possible.)

shiny	hot	tasty	nice	terrible	incredible	real
cold	long	extreme	important	festive	boring	awful

1. A morning in December	A morning in December is **terribly cold.**
2. A boring meeting	____________________
3. A summer holiday in Turkey	____________________
4. Long black hair	____________________
5. A good friend	____________________
6. Christmas	____________________
7. Football	____________________
8. A cheese cake	____________________

26. Use your adjectives correctly

Finish the sentences using the adjectives in the box.

disappointing/disappointed	depressing/depressed	boring/bored
amazing/amazed	exciting/excited	

1. The game wasn't as good as we had thought it would be, it was ______________.
2. Sue's going hand-gliding, it will be very ______________ for her.
3. He was ______________ when I said I wouldn't do it!
4. Rugby is ______________.
5. I was very ______________ with my performance.
6. It's been snowing all day. This weather is ______________.
7. Paul is ______________ because he can't find a girlfriend.
8. I'm ______________, let's go to town!
9. Claire is going to Africa next month, she is really ______________ about it.
10. John remembered your name? That's ______________.

27. Using the -ing form of the verb (with a future time) for fixed future plans

Write about your future fixed plans using the -ing form of the following verbs and a future time, as in the example.

go watch meet see eat play call

I **am going** on holiday **in June**.

1. ______________________________
2. ______________________________
3. ______________________________
4. ______________________________
5. ______________________________
6. ______________________________
7. ______________________________

28. Negative sentences practice

Use the words to write **negative sentences**, as in the examples.

I/play/tennis	I **don't** play tennis.
He/eat/meat	He **doesn't** eat meat.

1. She/watch/sport ______________________
2. I/like/him ______________________
3. Tom/travel/by car ______________________
4. He/walk/dog ______________________
5. Sue/like/flying ______________________
6. We/like/each other ______________________
7. They/talk/Russian ______________________
8. He/speak/Italian ______________________
9. I/see/film ______________________
10. He/call/Bob ______________________

29. Don't use the wrong verbs

Decide if these sentences are right or wrong. Correct them if necessary, as in the examples.

Paul made a big party.	Wrong! Paul **had** a big party.
Fred goes on holiday twice a year.	Right!

1. Shall I cook some coffee to wake us up? ______________________
2. If you do a mistake, correct it. ______________________
3. Let's make holiday in Spain this year. ______________________
4. I took hundreds of photos at the concert. ______________________
5. She spent her bonus to Oxfam. ______________________
6. When I saw Bill, he was driving a donkey. ______________________
7. Mum always stands up at five o'clock. ______________________
8. Do you look a lot of football? ______________________
9. Does your wife make a lot of sport? ______________________
10. I'm hearing my new CD. ______________________

30. Preference verbs

Complete the following sentences about yourself using the verbs in brackets, as in the example.

I like (watch) I **like watching** old films.

1. I like (eat) ______________________________
2. I don't like (play) ______________________________
3. I hate (clean) ______________________________
4. I don't mind (go) ______________________________
5. I love (meet) ______________________________

31. Simple present or present perfect?

Build questions with the words using either the simple present or the present perfect, as in the examples.

Do/live Where **do you** live?

How long/live How long **have you lived** there?

Where/work ______________________________

How long/work ______________________________

Do/sport ______________________________

Where/live/best friend ______________________________

How long/know ______________________________

32. 'Hear' or 'listen to'?

Complete the sentences using 'hear' or 'listen to'. Remember to use the correct tense.

1. I __________ the radio in my car.
2. My mum always __________ me when I come home late.
3. Didn't you __________ me?
4. Did you __________ the shouting last night?
5. I __________ a great opera on the radio yesterday.

6. Can you ____________ the children in their bedroom?
7. I ____________ the play on the radio.
8. Do you ever ____________ classical music?
9. I never ____________ him, he's boring.
10. Paul is ____________ music on his headphones.

33. 'Say' or 'tell'?

Finish these sentences using 'say' or 'tell' in the correct form.

1. My son always _______ me the truth.
2. Don't believe her, she always _______ lies.
3. _______ him to go away!
4. I _______ you yesterday.
5. She suddenly ______ everyone they had to leave.
6. Steve _______ me you lost your job?
7. Did she _______ hello to you?
8. Don't _______ me, you won!
9. What did your boss _______ about the accident?
10. What did you _____?

34. Office prepositions

Correct the prepositions, as in the example.

Paul is ~~in~~ the phone.	Paul is **on** the phone.
1. Steve is ~~on~~ a meeting.	____________________
2. I have a nice picture ~~at~~ my office wall.	____________________
3. I have to go ~~at~~ a meeting now.	____________________
4. Is Sally ~~on~~ the office today?	____________________
5. Have the report on my desk ~~until~~ Friday.	____________________
6. Bob's ~~in~~ holiday this week.	____________________
7. I spent all day working ~~to~~ the computer.	____________________

8. Put the new plant at the corner of the office. ______________________

9. The document you need is at my desk. ______________________

10. The new coffee machine is on the corridor. ______________________

35. Past perfect practice

Finish the sentences using the verb in brackets in the past perfect form (had + past participle), as in the example.

I saw the film 'Titanic' today, I **had never seen** it before.

1. I ate Sushi today, ______________________. (eat)
2. I met Pete's friend today, ______________________. (meet)
3. I saw a rat today, ______________________. (see)
4. I saw a French film today, ______________________. (see)
5. I went to visit Helen today, ______________________. (go out)
6. I went to Italy last year, ______________________. (be)
7. I saw Ted yesterday, ______________________. (break down)
8. I invited Tina to my party, ______________________. (make plans)
9. I saw a chimney yesterday, ______________________. (blow over)
10. I couldn't find my handbag, ______________________. (hide)

36. 'By' and 'until'

Decide if these sentences are right or wrong. Correct them if necessary, as in the examples.

I have to work by Friday.	Wrong! I have to work **until** Friday.
He should have been here by now!	Right!

1. Let's wait until it stops raining before we leave. ______________________
2. Make sure you are home until nine. ______________________
3. Let's wait until the prices fall before we buy. ______________________
4. You should have the money by the end of June. ______________________

5. I don't get paid until the 30th. ____________________
6. He didn't stop working by lunchtime. ____________________
7. I will be gone until the time you get back. ____________________
8. We must make a decision until tomorrow. ____________________
9. He's staying with me until he gets a new flat. ____________________
10. Make sure you're finished by lunchtime. ____________________

37. 'A' or 'an' practice

Put the correct article ('a' or 'an') next to the following words, leave the space blank if you think no article is needed, as in the examples.

an apple	a woman	an orange	___ weather
___ egg		___ igloo	___ cat
___ advice		___ hotel	___ dog
___ piece of information		___ car	___ icebox
___ elephant		___ progress	___ information

38. 'Same as' or 'like' or 'than'?

Complete the sentences using 'same as', 'like' or 'than', as in the example.

Paris is much bigger **than** Amsterdam.

1. ________ you, I don't like it.
2. Owning a house is the _______ having money in the bank.
3. He's just ________ his father!
4. Are you the _________ your brother?
5. I think I am taller ________ you.
6. This beer tastes the ________ the other one.
7. He's much smarter ________ you!
8. __________ David, I didn't study.
9. You can do better ________ that!
10. It's _________ déjà vu!

39. Simple past or past progressive?

Read this short text about Ralph, then answer the questions that follow using **the simple past** or **the past progressive**, as in the examples.

> *Yesterday I had a day off work. I got up just after seven, then I went for a long run until 10. When I got back I had a shower and drove to the city. At 12 o'clock I had an appointment with my dentist. At two o'clock I met my sister and we spent the rest of the afternoon at our father's house, who we hadn't seen for awhile.*

What time did Ralph get up?	He **got up** just after seven.
What was he doing at about half past eight?	He **was running** at half past eight.
1. When did he have a shower?	______________________
2. How did he get into the city?	______________________
3. What was he doing at about 12.15?	______________________
4. Who did he meet at two o'clock?	______________________
5. What was he doing in the afternoon?	______________________

40. 'Don't', 'doesn't', 'didn't' or 'not'?

Describe the situation on the left using 'don't', 'doesn't', 'didn't' or 'not', as in the examples.

1. John lives in his own apartment.	John **doesn't live** at home.
2. I have no interest in languages.	I **don't learn** any languages.
3. Paul has money in the bank.	______________________
4. I'm awake.	______________________
5. I started work straight after school.	______________________
6. Phil stayed in bed on Wednesday.	______________________
7. I'm a vegetarian.	______________________
8. She works part-time.	______________________
9. Paul hates sport.	______________________
10. I have a low-paid job.	______________________

41. Test your tenses

Complete the chart.

Simple present	**Simple past**	**Present progressive**	**Present perfect**
Things I do all the time.	*Finished actions.*	*What I am doing now. (temporary situations)*	*Up until now.*
I **live** in London.	I **lived** in London in 1992.	I **am living** in London until June.	I **have lived** in London.
	I **watched** TV last night.		
		I **am eating** sushi.	
	He **played** rugby on Saturday.		
		She **is writing** e-mails.	
			I **have done** my homework.

42. Test your plurals!

Write down the plurals of the following words:

bookshelf	____________	furniture	____________
man	____________	news	____________
mouse	____________	child	____________
party	____________	family	____________
woman	____________	mass	____________
hobby	____________	leaf	____________
foot	____________	knife	____________
aircraft	____________	information	____________
advice	____________	belief	____________
sheep	____________	housewife	____________
knowledge	____________	city	____________

43. 'A' and 'an' – exceptions practice

Decide if the following sentences are right or wrong. If you think they are wrong, correct them, as in the examples.

We stayed at an hotel.	Wrong! We stayed at **a** hotel.
Paul is an honest man.	Right!

1. Spain is an European country. ____________________
2. I need an new headlamp. ____________________
3. The euro is a unit of currency. ____________________
4. It was an honest mistake. ____________________
5. He's a one-company man. ____________________
6. It's an wonderful life. ____________________
7. It's a university course. ____________________
8. I need an orange and an apple. ____________________
9. He's an horrible man! ____________________
10. They put up a united front. ____________________

44. Get your tags right!

Finish the sentences by inserting the correct tag, as in the example.

This exercise is great, **isn't it**?

1. Tom won't be late, __________?
2. It's getting late, __________?
3. You couldn't lend me some money, __________?
4. I'm late, __________?
5. I don't look bad, __________?
6. I shouldn't have lost my temper, __________?
7. He'd never met her before, __________?
8. This jacket doesn't look very good on me, __________?
9. You earn a lot of money, __________?
10. There aren't many people here, __________?
11. That's just what you wanted, __________?
12. I'm too impatient, __________?

13. They will be late again, __________?
14. Barbara is beautiful, __________?
15. It wasn't me, __________?

45. Reflexive pronouns

Choose the correct reflexive pronoun to finish the sentences, as in the examples.

Bob's hurt **himself**.

She only thinks about **herself**.

1. The children look like they are really enjoying __________________.
2. Did you hurt ________________?
3. They are always gossiping amongst ____________________.
4. Don't worry, it will sort ______________ out!
5. I don't like him ______________.
6. We will decide for ______________.
7. He said he didn't need any help, let him do it _________________.
8. Sometimes I like to spoil __________________.
9. The chain wrapped _______________ around my wheel.
10. My parents are sunning _________________.

46. Adjectives & senses

Take **two words** from box A and **one word** from box B to make sentences. Remember to use the correct form, as in the example.

Box A			
smell	voice	material	coffee
feel	taste	meat	look
hairstyle	sound	tea	Susan

Box B		
bad	nice	terrible
soft	bitter	rough
good	fantastic	

This **coffee tastes nice**.

1. ______________________________
2. ______________________________
3. ______________________________
4. ______________________________
5. ______________________________
6. ______________________________

47. Will future or -ing form of the verb?

Write responses to the sentences on the right, using either will future or the -ing form of the verb, as in the examples.

What are you doing tonight, Tom?	**I'm watching** the big game on TV.
Dark clouds are forming in the sky.	I think **it will rain**.

1. I've got no money and it's only the 15th! ______________________
2. There is a crowd of people in the city centre. ______________________
3. We are playing the champions tonight. ______________________
4. Where are you going for your holidays? ______________________
5. What are you doing at the weekend? ______________________
6. The children are hungry. ______________________
7. Steve's girlfriend has left him. ______________________
8. You have an appointment at the doctor's. ______________________
9. You have no food in your fridge. ______________________
10. You booked a weekend in Paris for December. ______________________

48. Frequency adverbs

Take a frequency adverb from box A and an activity from box B and write sentences about yourself, as in the examples.

Box A		
sometimes	never	seldom
always	rarely	occasionally
often	usually	frequently

Box B

read books	cycle to work	eat fish
watch TV	listen to music	relax
phone friends	go hiking	play cards
play computer games	write letters	

I **rarely play** computer games.

I **sometimes listen to** music in the evening.

1. ______________________________
2. ______________________________
3. ______________________________
4. ______________________________
5. ______________________________
6. ______________________________
7. ______________________________
8. ______________________________
9. ______________________________
10. ______________________________

49. Using more than one adjective

Put the words in the right order to make sentences.

There/man/old/sad/is/ the/kitchen/in/a — There is a **sad, old** man in the kitchen.

1. big/table/round/a ______________________
2. scabby/cat/white/me/bit/a ______________________
3. cream/delicious/a/cake ______________________
4. bike/new/shiny/a ______________________
5. a/man/fat/sweaty ______________________

50. When to use 'the'

Complete the text below by choosing the correct words from the brackets.

One of my favourite cities is New York. I love the parks, especially ________________ (Central Park/the Central Park). I love to visit the theatres, which are mostly found near ________________ (Broadway/the Broadway). The best way to travel is by using ________________ (underground/the underground), the system is really modern. Another great place is ________________ (Soho/the Soho). It is the most amazing place. Of course, the best thing about New York is the shopping, (Macy's/the Macy's) is fantastic, but I prefer the markets in ________________ (Chelsea/the Chelsea). New York is a really expensive city. Last time I was there I stayed at ________________ (Hilton Hotel/the Hilton Hotel), I could only afford to stay one night, but it was a great experience.

51. Apostrophes

Correct these sentences by placing an apostrophe in the correct place, as in the examples.

I saw Jills new boyfriend last night.	I saw **Jill's** new boyfriend last night.
I went to my parents party last night.	I went to my **parents'** party last night.

1. Did you go to your nieces party on Sunday? ________________
2. Where is the womens toilet? ________________
3. Is that a childrens portion? ________________
4. That is last years model. ________________
5. Someone has smashed my neighbours window. ________________
6. My brothers wives are both French. ________________
7. I went to the dentists yesterday. ________________

8. Bob has been to the hairdressers. ______________________

9. I met my teachers husband yesterday. ______________________

10. There is a boys school on the corner. ______________________

52. Spelling exercises

a. Use a word in the box, in the correct form, to finish the sentences, as in the example.

country	baby	hobby	story	family	~~copy~~

I have two **copies** of the same magazine, would you like one?

1. He doesn't have many ____________.
2. He visited over 20 ______________ on his trip.
3. I always read bedtime ____________ to my children.
4. My grandma loves holding little ______________.
5. How many __________ live in your street?

b. Use a verb in the box, in the correct form, to finish the sentences, as in the example.

~~try~~	fry	cry	hurry	marry	study

He always **tries** to do his best.

1. He will be sorry if he _____________ her!
2. Paul is a good student, he _____________ very hard.
3. She ________ all the time.
4. If he __________, he'll catch the train.
5. He _________ all his food, it's so unhealthy.

53. Comparatives

Use the details below and the correct comparative to complete the sentences, as in the examples.

department store	shopping centre
Size: 25,000 square metres Rent: € 10 per square metre 40,000 customers per day Turnover: € 2.9 million a week	Size: 60,000 square metres Rent: € 15 per square metre 70,000 customers per day Turnover: € 6.3 million a week

1. The shopping centre is **bigger** than the department store.
2. The department store is **smaller** than the shopping centre.
3. The shopping centre's rent is ____________ than the department store's rent.
4. The department store has ____________ customers.
5. The shopping centre has a ____________ turnover than the department store.
6. The department store's turnover is ____________ the shopping centre's turnover.

54. 'To'/'too'/'two'

Use 'to', 'too' or 'two' to complete the text.

I was born in Leeds. I have _____ sisters, they were born there, _____. When I was 10, my family moved _____ Birmingham, but my father didn't like it. He said it was _____ loud and there were _____ many people. After four years we moved _____ a cottage in the country. It was nice, but _____ far away from our school. Every day I had to get _____ buses there and back. When I started work, I moved back _____ Leeds. I shared a flat with _____ friends for _____ years. The rent was _____ expensive but we were close _____ the city and the shops. When I got married we moved back _____ the country. I have _____ girls, they love it here.

55. Travel prepositions

Use the prepositions in the box to complete the sentences.

by	at	on	to	up	in

1. I went ____ the airport and picked ____ my mother.
2. Checking-____ can sometimes take hours.
3. When we got ____ passport control the queue was a mile long!
4. Prices ____ the airport are ridiculous.
5. My room was ____ the 22nd floor.
6. Lying ____ the beach or ____ the pool all day is really boring.
7. We found a nice bistro ____ a side street ____ the old town.
8. We travelled mostly ____ taxi, but sometimes we went ____ foot.
9. There was a beggar ____ every street corner!
10. I found an ice machine ____ the corridor of the hotel.

56. Past tense practice

Complete the sentences with the verb in brackets in the simple past.

1. Our company ______ a lot of money last year. (make)
2. I ______ my finger on the bread knife last night. (cut)
3. I ______ up at six o'clock. (get)
4. Steve ______ me a cup of tea. (bring)
5. I ______ for my holiday in Spain yesterday. (pay)
6. I really ______ the film on TV last night. (enjoy)
7. I ______ a new DVD on Saturday. (buy)
8. I ______ on the sofa all night and did nothing. (sit)
9. Steve ______ his coat on the bus. (leave)
10. I ______ a big bang in the night. (hear)
11. Bill ______ the ball. (catch)
12. I ______ the horror film on TV. (watch)

13. He ______ to me in French, but I ______ him. (speak/understand)

14. Paul ______ his arm playing football. (break)

15. It ______ to rain when I ______the house. (begin/leave)

16. I ______ a big breakfast, so I'm not hungry now. (eat)

17. I ______ the beer too quickly. (drink)

18. I ______to work. (drive)

19. I ______ all the way to my parents' house. (run)

20. I ______ to him on the telephone. (speak)

57. Present perfect practice

Re-write the sentences in the present perfect, as in the example.

Paul builds a house. Paul **has built** a house.

1. I choose a new dress. ____________________
2. Steve drives a big car. ____________________
3. I find some money. ____________________
4. The ship hits some rocks. ____________________
5. She hears the news. ____________________
6. We lose the game. ____________________
7. Do you see the cat? ____________________
8. Paul speaks to a French boy. ____________________
9. Ron swims in the sea. ____________________
10. He takes your coat. ____________________
11. We eat the cake. ____________________
12. Mum writes a letter to Paul. ____________________

58. 'There' or 'their'?

Complete the text using 'there' or 'their'.

_________ are a lot of ups and downs in my job. I work in a small company and I support our sales team. It is ________ job to market and sell our products all over the country.

_________ are lots of conferences to organise, hotels to book, and meetings to arrange.

One of my most important jobs is calculating and paying _________ travel expenses. The salesmen always want _________ money as quickly as possible. Last year _________ were a lot of redundancies because of the financial downturn and about 20 people lost ________ job.

59. Plurals practice

Choose the correct word to finish the sentences.

1. I need **a scissors/a pair of scissors** to cut the cardboard.
2. Those are **nice jeans/a nice jeans**!
3. Has anyone seen **my pyjamas/a pyjamas**?
4. I have two very sharp **knifes/knives**.
5. I need **new tights/a new tights**.
6. Did your husband put up the **shelves/shelfs**?
7. I can't see without **glasses/a glasses**.
8. He looks so silly in **big shorts/a big shorts**.
9. Don't you have **any nice trousers/a nice trousers**?
10. All the men are bringing their **wifes/wives**.

Exercise Answers

1. 'Do', 'make' or 'have'?

1. **Do** you like basketball?
2. I think he **does/has** a good job.
3. I'm getting tired, let's **make/have** some coffee to wake us up!
4. Are you **having** a party on your birthday?
5. Do you **do** much business with Japan?
6. They are **doing** some work on the street outside.
7. Who is **making** so much noise?
8. I'm hungry, let's **make/have** something to eat.
9. Tom **did** all the gardening yesterday.
10. Have you **done** your homework?
11. Dad can't come to the phone, he is **doing** the housework.
12. I can't believe I **made** so many mistakes in my test!
13. Have you ever **had** a fancy dress party?
14. They are **making** a huge cake for Dad's birthday.
15. I **did** my maths homework yesterday.
16. I always **do** my housework on Friday afternoon.
17. Did you **make** an appointment with the doctor?
18. Have you ever **made/had** Turkish pizza?
19. Did you **have** a nice holiday?
20. I don't like **doing** nothing, I get bored.

2. 'Look' or 'watch'?

1. Are you **looking** at me?
2. Are you **watching** me?
3. Do you **watch** a lot of sport on TV?
4. **Look** at that man! He's kicking his dog!
5. I **watched** the game last night.
6. Bill **looked** at the photo for a few seconds.
7. Did you **watch** the film last night?
8. I am **looking** for my watch, have you seen it?
9. I sometimes **watch** documentaries on TV.
10. Stop **looking** at your watch all the time!
11. Jack likes **watching** wrestling on TV.
12. The kids are playing hide and seek, they are **looking** for each other.

13. **Look** at the time! I must be going.
14. Hey, **look** where you are going!
15. Sue **watches** winter sport in the evening.
16. Don't disturb me, I'm **watching** my favourite programme.
17. I'm **looking** for a new job.
18. Paul was **looking** for his dog when I saw him last night.
19. I fell asleep while I was **watching** the debate.
20. Goodbye, **look** after yourself.

3. When and how to use 'have'

1. I have been to the cinema yesterday.	Wrong! I **went** to the cinema yesterday.
2. I have been to Spain many times.	Right!
3. Paul gone to lunch, he'll be back soon.	Wrong! Paul **has gone** to lunch, he'll be back soon.
4. I has made a birthday cake for Helen.	Wrong! I **have made** a birthday cake for Helen.
5. Pete has went to Spain.	Wrong! Pete **has gone** to Spain.
6. I have eaten Sushi many times.	Right!
7. Did you has a good time?	Wrong! Did you **have** a good time?
8. I have watched the game on Sunday.	Wrong! I **watched** the game on Sunday.
9. I eaten my lunch at twelve.	Wrong! I **ate** my lunch at twelve.
10. Steve has already did his homework.	Wrong! Steve has already **done** his homework.
11. I did my housework on Friday.	Right!
12. Are you has a party on Friday?	Wrong! Are you **having** a party on Friday?
13. Did you has a good holiday?	Wrong! Did you **have** a good holiday?
14. I'm having a break.	Right!
15. She has been to the doctor's.	Right!
16. I went to work on Saturday.	Right!
17. I'm have a day off tomorrow.	Wrong! I'm **having** a day off tomorrow.
18. Steve had two days off after his crash.	Right!
19. Has you any brothers and sisters?	Wrong! Do you **have** any brothers and sisters?
20. They has no idea what they are doing!	Wrong! They **have** no idea what they are doing!

4. 'At' or 'with'?

1. I was **at** my sister's.
2. He is living **with** Pete until he finds his own place.
3. She was **at** the hairdresser's for hours!
4. He's over forty, but he still lives **with** his parents!
5. I am not sure where he is, I think he's **with** his brother.
6. She's **at** the doctor's.
7. He's gone on holiday **with** his parents.
8. She is living **with** him.
9. I am staying **with** Jill while my flat is being renovated.
10. She's **with** Phil, I think!

5. 'Many' or 'much'?

a.

how many	**how much**
children	meat
people	sand
hands	progress
jobs	homework
teeth	housework
roads	money
men	work
feet	traffic

b.

1. How **much** progress did you make in the meeting?
2. Does your English teacher give you **much** homework?
3. How **much** housework do you have to do this weekend?
4. Paul put too **much** sand in with the concrete mix.
5. There is always so **much** traffic on the motorways.
6. How **many** children do you have?
7. How **many** jobs does she have?
8. How **much** money will you need to buy the house?
9. How **many** men were needed for the work?
10. How **much** work did you do on the house on Sunday?

6. Don't Germanise it!

1. I need an electriker.	Wrong! I need **an electrician**.
2. See you tomorrow!	Right!
3. Mum said me I was good.	Wrong! Mum **told me** I was good.
4. How was your travel to France?	Wrong! How was your **journey/trip** to France?
5. One of my friend is ill.	Wrong! One of my **friends** is ill.
6. Are you good in tennis?	Wrong! Are you good **at** tennis?
7. I was on a party last night.	Wrong! I was **at** a party last night.
8. There's Steve! He's the husband of my sister.	Wrong! There's Steve! He's my **sister's** husband.
9. Let's have a party!	Right!
10. Tom's on a meeting.	Wrong! Tom's **in/at** a meeting.

7. Countable or uncountable?

man	men	woman	women
child	children	road	roads
knowledge	knowledge	information	information
bread	bread	roll	rolls
knife	knives	person	people
keyboard	keyboards	advice	advice
homework	homework	news	news

8. Vocabulary

a.

Spülmaschine	dishwasher
sympathisch	nice/pleasant
Aufenthaltserlaubnis	residence permit
Hochzeitstag	wedding anniversary
Mehrwertsteuer	Value Added Tax (VAT)
Waschmaschine	washing machine
Beratung	advice
Mutterschaftsurlaub	maternity leave
Kindergeld	child allowance
Fangfrage	trick question

b.
1. If you need good financial **advice**, ask Bob.
2. She spends all the **child allowance** on herself!
3. The rate of **VAT** has gone up again.
4. When is your **wedding anniversary**?
5. Is that **a trick question**?
6. My **residence permit** runs out at the end of the year.
7. Is your boss **nice**?
8. The **washing machine** is broken, I don't have any clean clothes!
9. The **dishwasher** is full.
10. She took 12 months **maternity leave** after her son was born.

9. Countries & languages

Belgium	Belgian	Russia	Russian
Holland	Dutch	Canada	Canadian
Spain	Spanish	Italy	Italian
Iceland	Icelandic	Pakistan	Pakistani
Israel	Israeli	Kenya	Kenyan

10. Adjectives and adverbs

1. I like him, he's **nice**.
2. She sings so **beautifully**.
3. The match was so **exciting**.
4. Are you **tired**?
5. He spoke very **nicely** to the children.
6. She shouted **loudly** at the child.
7. We completed the deal **successfully**.
8. He ran home **quickly**.
9. He stretched **tiredly**.
10. Are you sitting **comfortably**?

11. Word order

1. Do you have any **brothers** and **sisters**?
2. They are so different, they are like **chalk** and **cheese**!
3. It doesn't matter if you are **rich** or **poor**, just be healthy.
4. **Ladies** and **gentlemen**, welcome to the show!
5. Who is going to clean all the **pots** and **pans**?

6. She is so nosy, she wants to know the **ins** and **outs** of everything!
7. That film is old, it's in **black** and **white**.
8. The **boys** and **girls** have gone out to play.
9. It's raining **cats** and **dogs**.
10. I like reading novels about **kings** and **queens** of old England.

12. Nouns and verbs

a.

Noun	Verb
protection	(to) protect
mixture	**(to) mix**
correction	(to) correct
provision	(to) provide
taxation	**(to) tax**
imagination	**(to) imagine**
proof	(to) prove
composition	**(to) compose**
difference	**(to) differ**
description	**(to) describe**

b.

1. The police knew he was guilty, but they couldn't **prove** it.
2. 45 % **taxation** on salaries is too high.
3. Tom got his test back from the teacher and it was full of **corrections.**
4. All our production workers have to wear goggles for **protection**.
5. Does your company **provide** any leisure facilities?
6. John has just **composed** a new song.
7. We couldn't agree, so we agreed to **differ**!
8. **Mix** the cement in a bucket.
9. The officers have a good **description** of the criminal.
10. She is always **correcting** my English!

13. General prepositions

1. I am very good **at** badminton.
2. She got married **at** the age of 25.
3. He's married **to** a model.
4. Let's go to the hotel **on** foot.

5. My kitchen is 8 metres **by** 3 metres.
6. Can you look **after** my dog for a week?
7. I have to finish this job **by** Friday.
8. My hometown is west **of** Manchester.
9. **In** the short-term it's a bad plan.
10. Why not go **on** your own?

14. Don't say too much!

1. He's staying in a five-stars hotel.	Wrong! He's staying in a **five-star** hotel.
2. She has a two-years-old child.	Wrong! She has a **two-year-old** child.
3. It is almost 10 o'clock p.m.	Wrong! It is almost **10 p.m.**
4. He was given a five-year contract.	Right!
5. Are you going for a lunch with Jack?	Wrong! Are you going **for lunch** with Jack?
6. Our hotel has five stars.	Right!
7. He's coming the month after next.	Right!
8. Are you going home?	Right!
9. Did you go to the work yesterday?	Wrong! Did you go **to work** yesterday?
10. We had a breakfast in bed.	Wrong! We had **breakfast** in bed.

15. Get your expressions right!

1. What do you usually do on a Sunday morning?	I usually have **a lie-in**.
2. What do most people do during the week?	They **get up** for work.
3. What do you do when you're hungry?	I **make** something to eat.
4. How do you keep fit?	I **do** sport.
5. What do you do when you are feeling lazy?	I **do** nothing.

16. 'At' or 'by'?

1. We saw him **at** the cinema.
2. Have you been **at** the hairdresser's?
3. We went **by** taxi.
4. He's **at** his mother's.
5. He's staying **at** a really nice hotel.
6. Do you live **by** the river?

7. He should be here **by** now!
8. **By** the way, you still owe me €50!
9. He did it all **by** himself.
10. **By** the time I get to Phoenix, she'll be sleeping.

17. To be or not to be?

1. Did you go to work yesterday?	Right!
2. When are you going to home?	Wrong! When are you **going home**?
3. Did you go to holiday last summer?	Wrong! Did you go **on holiday** last summer?
4. Shall we go to a nice restaurant tonight?	Right!
5. I'm going to bed.	Right!

18. Don't translate word for word!

1. On the one **hand**, it's a great idea. On the other **hand**, it's dangerous.
2. The banks make huge **profits** at the expense of their customers.
3. I always **donate** money to Oxfam at Christmas.
4. Do you **spend** a lot of money **on** birthday presents?
5. You found €50? You are so **lucky**.
6. I am **happy** with my figure.
7. Did you **get** my message?
8. What has **become** of Tom? I haven't seen him for months!
9. Put the address on the **back** of the parcel, too!
10. Are you any good **at** chess?

19. 'During' and 'while'

1. He learned a lot **during** his time in the army.
2. I like to drink a glass of wine **while** I'm cooking.
3. The telephone rang **while** I was having a shower.
4. When I saw Tom he was waiting for a bus **while** he was reading a book.
5. **During** the conference I did a lot of networking.
6. Will you visit Harry **during** your US trip?
7. Don't talk **while** you're eating.
8. They repair your shoes **while** you wait.
9. I relaxed **during** the weekend.
10. I can't sleep **during** the day.

20 'Look after' and 'look for'?

1. Sue is fed up at work, she is **looking for** a new job.
2. He always **looks for** the cheapest hotels.
3. He **looked for** a new flat last week.
4. I'm **looking after** my parents' dog while they are in France.
5. I **look for** the best deals on the internet.
6. He **looks after** his health.
7. I'm **looking for** my cat, have you seen it?
8. He **looked after** his mother for two years when she was sick.
9. They really **look after** their customers.
10. I've **looked for** my keys everywhere. I can't find them!

21. Prefixes

possible	**impossible**	modest	**immodest**
polite	**impolite**	regular	**irregular**
secure	**insecure**	safe	**unsafe**
mobile	**immobile**	trustworthy	**untrustworthy**
appear	**disappear**	expected	**unexpected**
well	**unwell**	attractive	**unattractive**
relevant	**irrelevant**	able	**unable**
organised	**disorganised**	treated	**untreated**
believable	**unbelievable**	happy	**unhappy**
responsible	**irresponsible**	mature	**immature**
sure	**unsure**	reasonable	**unreasonable**

22. 'There is'/'there are'

1. **There is** no point waiting, he'll be another three hours.
2. I know where **there are** more biscuits!
3. She said **there are** many problems in her relationship.
4. **There are** a lot of dogs in the park.
5. I know **there is** something going on!
6. **There was** only one till open at the check-out yesterday.
7. **There is** a lot of noise coming from Joe's room.
8. **There were** thunderstorms last night.
9. **There are** not enough hotels in the city.
10. **There is** no infrastructure in our country.

23. Time prepositions

1. Shall we have a party **on** my birthday?
2. We can meet **next Tuesday**.
3. I saw Bob **last week**.
4. I play tennis **on** Sunday.
5. I have been working here **for** 10 years.
6. Did you go to church **on** Easter Sunday?
7. Did it snow **at** Christmas?
8. The cat always goes out **at** night.
9. Did you see your mother **on** Christmas Day?
10. The ambulance arrived **in** five minutes.

24. 'Who' and 'which' (Possible answers)

1. **A nurse** is someone **who** looks after sick people.
2. **A teacher** is a person **who** teaches children.
3. **A bat** is a creature **which** only comes out at night.
4. **Smoking** is something **which** is very bad for your health.
5. **Your best friend** is someone **who** you can rely on.
6. **Steak** is something **which** costs a lot of money.
7. **History** is a subject **which** I'm very interested in.
8. **Chess** is a game **which** clever people play.
9. **A policeman** is someone **who** catches criminals.
10. **A car** is something **which** you use to get around.

25. Using an adverb to describe an adjective (Possible answers)

1.	A morning in December	A morning in December is **terribly cold**.
2.	A boring meeting	A boring meeting can be **awfully long**.
3.	A summer holiday in Turkey	A summer holiday in Turkey is **incredibly hot**.
4.	Long black hair	Long black hair is **really shiny**.
5.	A good friend	A good friend is **extremely important**.
6.	Christmas	Christmas is **incredibly festive**.
7.	Football	Football is **extremely boring**.
8.	A cheese cake	A cheese cake is **really tasty**.

26. Use your adjectives correctly!

1. The game wasn't as good as we had thought it would be, it was **disappointing**.
2. Sue's going hand-gliding, it will be very **exciting** for her.
3. He was **amazed** when I said I wouldn't do it!
4. Rugby is **boring**.
5. I was very **disappointed** with my performance.
6. It's been snowing all day. This weather is **depressing**.
7. Paul is **depressed** because he can't find a girlfriend.
8. I'm **bored**, let's go to town!
9. Claire is going to Africa next month, she is really **excited** about it.
10. John remembered your name? That's **amazing**.

27. Using the -ing form of the verb (with a future time) for fixed future plans (Possible answers)

1. I **am going** to bed early **tonight**.
2. I **am watching** the big match **tomorrow**.
3. I **am meeting** Jim for a coffee **at lunchtime**.
4. I **am seeing** my mother **at the weekend**.
5. I **am eating** at the new restaurant **tonight**.
6. I **am playing** basketball **on Friday**.
7. I **am calling** Helen **tonight**.

28. Negative sentences practice

1. She **doesn't** watch sport.
2. I **don't** like him.
3. Tom **doesn't** travel by car.
4. He **doesn't** walk the/his dog.
5. Sue **doesn't** like flying.
6. We **don't** like each other.
7. They **don't** talk Russian.
8. He **doesn't** speak Italian.
9. I **don't** see the film.
10. He **doesn't** call Bob.

29. Don't use the wrong verbs!

1. Shall I cook some coffee to wake us up?	Wrong! Shall I **make** some coffee to wake us up?
2. If you do a mistake, correct it.	Wrong! If you **make** a mistake, correct it.
3. Let's make holiday in Spain this year.	Wrong! Let's **go on** holiday **to** Spain this year.
4. I took hundreds of photos at the concert.	Right!
5. She spent her bonus to Oxfam.	Wrong! She **donated** her bonus to Oxfam.
6. When I saw Bill, he was driving a donkey.	Wrong! When I saw Bill, he was **riding** a donkey.
7. Mum always stands up at five o'clock.	Wrong! Mum always **gets up** at five o'clock.
8. Do you look a lot of football?	Wrong! Do you **watch** a lot of football?
9. Does your wife make a lot of sport?	Wrong! Does your wife **do** a lot of sport?
10. I'm hearing my new CD.	Wrong! I'm **listening to** my new CD.

30. Preference verbs (Possible answers)

1. I **like eating** fish.
2. I don't **like playing** chess.
3. I **hate cleaning** windows.
4. I **don't mind going** to my sister's.
5. I **love meeting** new people.

31. Simple present or present perfect? (Possible answers)

1. Where **do** you **work**?
2. How long **have you worked** there?
3. **Do** you **do** sport?
4. Where **does** your best friend **live**?
5. How long **have you known** him/her?

32. ‘Hear’ or ‘listen to’?

1. I **listen to** the radio in my car.
2. My mum always **hears** me when I come home late.
3. Didn’t you **hear** me?
4. Did you **hear** the shouting last night?
5. I **heard/listened to** a great opera on the radio yesterday.
6. Can you **hear** the children in their bedroom?
7. I **listened to** the play on the radio.
8. Do you ever **listen to** classical music?
9. I never **listen to** him, he’s boring.
10. Paul is **listening to** music on his headphones.

33. ‘Say’ or ‘tell’?

1. My son always **tells** me the truth.
2. Don’t believe her, she always **tells** lies.
3. **Tell** him to go away!
4. I **told** you yesterday.
5. She suddenly **told** everyone they had to leave.
6. Steve **told** me you lost your job?
7. Did she **say** hello to you?
8. Don’t **tell** me, you won!
9. What did your boss **say** about the accident?
10. What did you **say**?

34. Office prepositions

1. Steve is **in/at** a meeting.
2. I have a nice picture **on** my office wall.
3. I have to go **to** a meeting now.
4. Is Sally **in** the office today?
5. Have the report on my desk **by** Friday.
6. Bob’s **on** holiday this week.
7. I spent all day working **on** the computer.
8. Put the new plant **in** the corner of the office.
9. The document you need is **on** my desk.
10. The new coffee machine is **in** the corridor.

35. Past perfect practice (Possible answers)

1. I ate Sushi today, I **had never eaten** it before.
2. I met Pete's friend today, I **had never met** him before.
3. I saw a rat today, I **had never seen** a rat before.
4. I saw a French film today, I **had seen** it before.
5. I went to visit Helen today, but she **had gone out**.
6. I went to Italy last year, I **had been there** many times before.
7. I saw Ted yesterday, he **had broken down**.
8. I invited Tina to my party, but she **had already made** other plans.
9. I saw a chimney yesterday, it **had blown** over.
10. I couldn't find my handbag, someone **had hidden** it.

36. 'By' and 'until'

1. Let's wait until it stops raining before we leave.	Right!
2. Make sure you are home until nine.	Wrong! **By** nine.
3. Let's wait until the prices fall before we buy.	Right!
4. You should have the money by the end of June.	Right!
5. I don't get paid until the 30th.	Right!
6. He didn't stop working by lunchtime.	Wrong! **Until** lunchtime.
7. I will be gone until the time you get back.	Wrong! **By** the time you get back.
8. We must make a decision until tomorrow.	Wrong! **By** tomorrow.
9. He's staying with me until he gets a new flat.	Right!
10. Make sure you're finished by lunchtime.	Right!

37. 'A' or 'an' practice

an egg	**an** igloo	**a** cat
advice	**a** hotel	**a** dog
a piece of information	**a** car	**an** icebox
an elephant	progress	information

38. 'Same as' or 'like' or 'than'?

1. **Same as** you, I don't like it.
2. Owning a house is the **same as** having money in the bank.
3. He's just **like** his father!
4. Are you the **same as** your brother?

5. I think I am taller **than** you.
6. This beer tastes the **same as** the other one.
7. He's much smarter **than** you!
8. **Like** David, I didn't study.
9. You can do better **than** that!
10. It's **like** déjà vu!

39. Simple past or past progressive?

1. He **had** a shower at 10.
2. He **drove** to the city.
3. He was **sitting** in the dentist's chair.
4. He **met** his sister.
5. He **was visiting** his father.

40. 'Don't', 'doesn't', 'didn't' or 'not'?
(Possible answers)

1. John lives in his own apartment.	John **doesn't live** at home.
2. I have no interest in languages.	I **don't learn** any languages.
3. Paul has money in the bank.	Paul **doesn't owe** any money.
4. I'm awake.	I'm **not sleeping**.
5. I started work straight after school.	I **didn't study** at university.
6. Phil stayed in bed on Wednesday.	Phil **didn't go** to work on Wednesday.
7. I'm a vegetarian.	I **don't eat** meat.
8. She works part-time.	She **doesn't have** a full-time job.
9. Paul hates sport.	Paul **doesn't do** sport.
10. I have a low-paid job.	I **don't earn** much money.

41. Test your tenses

Simple present	**Simple past**	**Present progressive**	**Present perfect**
Things I do all the time.	*Finished actions.*	*What I am doing now. (temporary situations)*	*Up until now.*
I **live** in London.	I **lived** in London in 1992.	I **am living** in London until June.	I **have lived** in London.
I **watch** TV.	I **watched** TV last night.	I **am watching** TV.	I **have watched** TV.
I **eat** sushi.	I **ate** sushi last Saturday.	I **am eating** sushi.	I **have eaten** sushi.
He **plays** rugby.	He **played** rugby on Saturday.	He **is playing** rugby.	He **has played** rugby.
She **writes** e-mails.	She **wrote** e-mails yesterday.	She **is writing** e-mails.	She **has written** e-mails.
I **do** my homework on Sundays.	I **did** my homework on Sunday.	I **am doing** my homework.	I **have done** my homework.

42. Test your plurals!

bookshelf	bookshelves	furniture	furniture
man	men	news	news
mouse	mice	child	children
party	parties	family	families
woman	women	mass	masses
hobby	hobbies	leaf	leaves
foot	feet	knife	knives
aircraft	aircraft	information	information
advice	advice	belief	beliefs
sheep	sheep	housewife	housewives
knowledge	knowledge	city	cities

43. 'A' and 'an' – exceptions practice

1. Spain is an European country. Wrong! Spain is **a** European country.
2. I need an new headlamp. Wrong! I need **a** new headlamp.

3. The euro is a unit of currency. Right!
4. It was an honest mistake. Right!
5. He's a one-company man. Right!
6. It's an wonderful life. Wrong! It's **a** wonderful life.
7. It's a university course. Right!
8. I need an orange and an apple. Right!
9. He's an horrible man! Wrong! He's **a** horrible man!
10. They put up a united front. Right!

44. Get your tags right

1. Tom won't be late, **will he**?
2. It's getting late, **isn't it**?
3. You couldn't lend me some money, **could you**?
4. I'm late, **aren't I**?
5. I don't look bad, **do I**?
6. I shouldn't have lost my temper, **should I**?
7. He'd never met her before, **had he**?
8. This jacket doesn't look very good on me, **does it**?
9. You earn a lot of money, **don't you**?
10. There aren't many people here, **are there**?
11. That's just what you wanted, **isn't it**?
12. I'm too impatient, **aren't I**?
13. They will be late again, **won't they**?
14. Barbara is beautiful, **isn't she**?
15. It wasn't me, **was it**?

45. Reflexive pronouns

1. The children look like they are really enjoying **themselves**.
2. Did you hurt **yourself**?
3. They are always gossiping amongst **themselves**.
4. Don't worry, it will sort **itself** out!
5. I don't like him **myself**.
6. We will decide for **ourselves**.
7. He said he didn't need any help, let him do it **himself**.
8. Sometimes I like to spoil **myself**.
9. The chain wrapped **itself** around my wheel.
10. My parents are sunning **themselves**.

46. Adjectives & senses (Possible answers)

1. This **meat smells bad**.
2. This **material feels soft**.
3. This **tea tastes bitter**.
4. Your **hairstyle looks fantastic**.
5. Susan **smells terrible**.
6. Your **voice sounds rough**.

47. Will future or -ing form of the verb? (Possible answers)

1.	I've got no money and it's only the 15th!	It's ok, I **will lend** you some.
2.	There is a crowd of people in the city centre.	I think there **will be** trouble.
3.	We are playing the champions tonight.	I think you **will lose**.
4.	Where are you going for your holidays?	I **am going** to Scotland.
5.	What are you doing at the weekend?	I **am doing** nothing special.
6.	The children are hungry.	I **will make** them something to eat.
7.	Steve's girlfriend has left him.	I think he **will be** sad.
8.	You have an appointment at the doctor's.	I **am going** to the doctor's tomorrow.
9.	You have no food in your fridge.	I **will go** shopping.
10.	You booked a weekend in Paris for December.	I **am going** to Paris in December.

48. Frequency adverbs (Possible answers)

1. I **always** read books.
2. I **rarely** go hiking.
3. I **often** play computer games.
4. I **never** eat fish.
5. I **usually** cycle to work.
6. I **seldom** write letters.
7. I **frequently** listen to music.
8. I **sometimes** watch TV.
9. I **occasionally** phone friends.
10. I **often** relax.

49. Using more than one adjective (Possible answers)

1. They bought a **big, round** table.
2. A **scabby, white** cat bit me.
3. I want to eat a **delicious cream** cake.
4. He got a **shiny, new** bike.
5. A **sweaty, fat** man sat down right next to me.

50. When to use 'the'

One of my favourite cities is New York. I love the parks, especially **Central Park**. I love to visit the theatres, which are mostly found near **Broadway**. The best way to travel is by using **the underground**, the system is really modern. Another great place is **Soho**. It is the most amazing place. Of course, the best thing about New York is the shopping, **Macy's** is fantastic, but I prefer the markets in **Chelsea**. New York is a really expensive city. Last time I was there I stayed at **the Hilton Hotel**, I could only afford to stay one night, but it was a great experience.

51. Apostrophes

1. Did you go to your **niece's/nieces'** party on Sunday?
2. Where is the **women's** toilet?
3. Is that a **children's** portion?
4. That is last **year's** model.
5. Someone has smashed my **neighbour's/neighbours'** window.
6. My **brothers'** wives are both French.
7. I went to the **dentist's** yesterday.
8. Bob has been to the **hairdresser's**.
9. I met my **teacher's** husband yesterday.
10. There is a **boys'** school on the corner.

52. Spelling exercises

a.

1. He doesn't have many **hobbies**.
2. He visited over 20 **countries** on his trip.
3. I always read bedtime **stories** to my children.
4. My grandma loves holding little **babies**.
5. How many **families** live in your street?

b.
1. He will be sorry if he **marries** her!
2. Paul is a good student, he **studies** very hard.
3. She **cries** all the time.
4. If he **hurries**, he'll catch the train.
5. He **fries** all his food, it's so unhealthy.

53. Comparatives

1. The shopping centre is **bigger** than the department store.
2. The department store is **smaller** than the shopping centre.
3. The shopping centre's rent is **higher** than the department store's rent.
4. The department store has **fewer** customers.
5. The shopping centre has a **higher** turnover than the department store.
6. The department store's turnover is **lower** than the shopping centre's turnover.

54. 'To'/'too'/'two'

I was born in Leeds. I have **two** sisters, they were born there, **too**. When I was 10, my family moved **to** Birmingham, but my father didn't like it. He said it was **too** loud and there were **too** many people. After four years we moved **to** a cottage in the country. It was nice, but **too** far away from our school. Every day I had to get **two** buses there and back. When I started work, I moved back **to** Leeds. I shared a flat with **two** friends for **two** years. The rent was **too** expensive but we were close **to** the city and the shops. When I got married we moved back **to** the country. I have **two** girls, they love it here.

55. Travel prepositions

1. I went **to** the airport and picked **up** my mother.
2. Checking-**in** can sometimes take hours.
3. When we got **to** passport control the queue was a mile long!
4. Prices **at** the airport are ridiculous.
5. My room was **on** the 22nd floor.
6. Lying **on** the beach or **by** the pool all day is really boring.
7. We found a nice bistro **in** a side street **in** the old town.
8. We travelled mostly **by** taxi, but sometimes we went **on** foot.
9. There was a beggar **on** every street corner!
10. I found an ice machine **in** the corridor of the hotel.

56. Past tense practice

1. Our company **made** a lot of money last year.
2. I **cut** my finger on the bread knife last night.
3. I **got** up at six o'clock.
4. Steve **brought** me a cup of tea.
5. I **paid** for my holiday in Spain yesterday.
6. I really **enjoyed** the film on TV last night.
7. I **bought** a new DVD on Saturday.
8. I **sat** on the sofa all night and did nothing.
9. Steve **left** his coat on the bus.
10. I **heard** a big bang in the night.
11. Bill **caught** the ball.
12. I **watched** the horror film on TV.
13. He **spoke** to me in French, but I **understood** him.
14. Paul **broke** his arm playing football.
15. It **began** to rain when I **left** the house.
16. I **ate** a big breakfast, so I'm not hungry now.
17. I **drank** the beer too quickly.
18. I **drove** to work.
19. I **ran** all the way to my parents' house.
20. I **spoke** to him on the telephone.

57. Present perfect practice

1. I **have chosen** a new dress.
2. Steve **has driven** a big car.
3. I **have found** some money.
4. The ship **has hit** some rocks.
5. She **has heard** the news.
6. We **have lost** the game.
7. **Have you seen** the cat?
8. Paul **has spoken** to a French boy.
9. Ron **has swum** in the sea.
10. He **has taken** your coat.
11. We **have eaten** the cake.
12. Mum **has written** a letter to Paul.

58. ‘There’ or ‘their’?

There are a lot of ups and downs in my job. I work in a small company and I support our sales team. It is **their** job to market and sell our products all over the country.

There are lots of conferences to organise, hotels to book, and meetings to arrange.

One of my most important jobs is calculating and paying **their** travel expenses. The salesmen always want **their** money as quickly as possible. Last year **there** were a lot of redundancies because of the financial downturn and about 20 people lost **their** job.

59. Plurals practice

1. I need **a pair of scissors** to cut the cardboard.
2. Those are **nice jeans**!
3. Has anyone seen my **pyjamas**?
4. I have two very sharp **knives**.
5. I need new **tights**.
6. Did your husband put up the **shelves**?
7. I can’t see without **glasses**.
8. He looks so silly in **big shorts**.
9. Don’t you have any nice **trousers**?
10. All the men are bringing their **wives**.